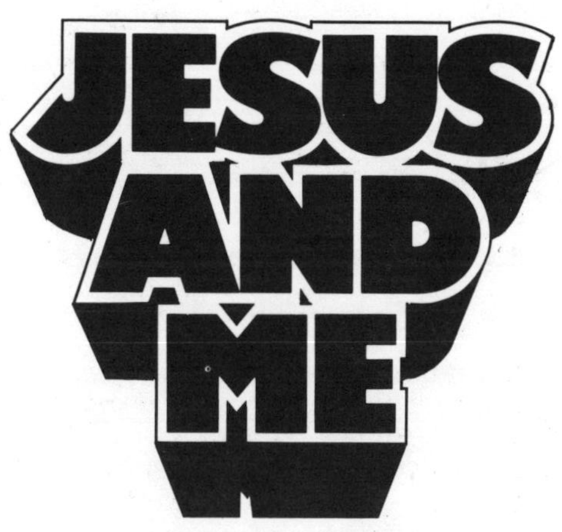

Gladys Seashore

His International Service
Minneapolis, Minnesota 55423

Published by His International Service
Minneapolis, Minn. 55423

ISBN 0-911802-37-1

Scripture quotations from *The Living Bible* © 1971 Tyndale House Publishers, Wheaton, IL are used by permission of the publishers.

Games We Play, pages 22, 27, 31, 35, 39, 42 and 48, by Jim Smoke, adapted from Campus Life, © 1968, Youth For Christ International. Used by permission.

Photography on pages 8, 24, 29, 33, 36, 40, 50 and 58, by *H. Armstrong Roberts*; pages 14 and 20 by *Jim Whitmer*; page 44 by *Harold M. Lambert* and page 54 by *Orville Andrews*.

Every effort has been made to identify and acknowledge the source of all material used. Material presently unidentified will be acknowledged in subsequent editions as information is received.

*To
My Sons*

CONTENTS

INTRODUCTION

Life is a challenge. As in the days of the pioneers, those heading west had great plains to cross, rivers to ford, and mountains to climb, before claiming their homestead rights, so Christians today have many obstacles to overcome before we finally reach "Home." But *we don't face life alone!* God's Word is a lamp for our feet and a light for our path. My purpose in this study is to turn the spotlight of God's Word on some of the troublesome areas in the lives of youth to help you over a few of the rough spots.

Before you dig in, I would like to make a few suggestions. This book was prepared for small group discussions, but it is adaptable for individual devotions, taking one or two sections a day. If you are unfamiliar with the Bible, the book is given first (find it in the index), then the chapter and the verse. For instance, John 1:12. Find the book of John, the first chapter and the twelfth verse. I have used three of the more popular versions in my study. The familiar *King James Version, Today's English Version,* more often known as *Good News for Modern Man,* and *The Living Bible,* the popular paraphrase by Kenneth Taylor.

Now a word to discussion leaders. Don't hurry through a lesson. Leave time for discussion, but when that discussion begins to ramble, tactfully bring the group back to the matter at hand. Avoid being dogmatic. Lead your young people to the Word and let the Word work. Don't try to lead a group without carefully preparing in advance, both by study and prayer.

The song, *Jesus And Me,* by Ira F. Stanphill, *(Favorites #6,* Singspiration, Inc., p. 35) is ideal for use with this study, accenting vital truth and adding a bright, cheerful worship experience when used at the beginning of each class session.

My prayer is that this little book will help someone find the Way a little easier. Have a good trip.

A SPECIAL ME

I. I AM VERY SPECIAL TO GOD
   A. When did this begin? Psalm 139:13-18

   B. How much does God love me?
      1. *John 3:16*

      2. *I John 4:9,10*

II. I AM VERY SPECIAL TO JESUS CHRIST
   A. How much does Jesus love me? John 15:9

   B. What price did Jesus have to pay for His love?
      1. *John 15:13*

      2. *Romans 5:8*

      3. *John 10:17,18*

   C. In what way does He show His love?
      1. *John 1:12*

      2. *I John 3:1*

III. SPECIAL BLESSINGS GOD GIVES HIS CHILDREN
   A. What new things does He give us when we receive Jesus
      Christ as our personal Saviour and thus become God's child?
      1. *Revelation 2:17; 3:12*

      2. *Revelation 19:8; Isaiah 61:10*

         What were our old ones like? Isaiah 64:6

      3. *Psalm 40:3*

4. *II Corinthians 5:17*

B. How can I become God's child?

   1. *As we are born physically, we must be born spiritually. Read John 3:1-17. What kind of a man do you think Nicodemus was?*

   2. *Of whom are we born the second time? John 3:3-7*

   3. *What is our part? What is His part?*
      I John 1:8,9

      John 1:12

      Revelation 3:20

      Romans 10:9,10

Have you received Jesus Christ as your personal Saviour and become HIS VERY OWN?

Who am I, God,
Who am I?
Sometimes I wonder
Deep in this soul of mine
Who am I?

Where am I, God,
Where am I?
Sometimes I wonder
Deep in this soul of mine,
Where am I?

Why am I, God,
Why am I?
Sometimes I wonder
Deep in this soul of mine
Why am I, God?

—Gladys Seashore

TWO WORLDS

God made a world,
And in it there are
mountains,
Sunbeams and roses,
And towering pines above
Cascades and falls,
And rippling brooks and
fountains,
All of them telling of God,
His power and love.

Man made a world,
And it was dark and
smoky,
Crowded with poverty,
Greed and soul despair—
Mankind enslaving man,
And all his day-dreams
wrecking—
Piling his back and heart
With burdens hard to
bear.

God made a world
All full of fruit and
flowers,
Crystalline moonbeams,
And a baby's smile.
Man made a world
Unclean, corrupt, and
fetid—
With slimy wiles
To make that baby vile.

God's world is good
And only man is evil.
God's Word is true
And man alone can lie.
Shall God be blamed
Because man is a failure?
Who shall accuse
When man makes choice
to die?

—Will H. Houghton

I WOULD LEARN OF THIS POWER

by Lois F. Reed

Suppose the universe is one big coincidence,
    the accidental meeting in space of two or three or
    four gases, combining and reacting
    and forming the earth and stars.
Suppose too that man is coincidence,
    the accidental combination of gases
    evolving over the centuries
    into the complex multicellular human form.
Pursue the pattern of coincidence
    to account for all existence, and explain to me
    joy, despair, rapture, aspiration
    in the unexplained tingling that floods through me.
Tell me how isolated sounds are accidentally put together
    to make music.
Assure me that the soul's song in the presence of beauty
    is only the action and reaction
    of muscles and nerves.
Explain to me the scientific phenomena
    underlying the power that causes men
    to do incredible things for the sake of another,
    the power and fact called love.
I would learn of this power,
    for without it each man is no more
    than an excellent physiological unit,
    capable of perceiving only
    that ages grind relentlessly for nothing.
Is love another coincidence,
    enzymes or proteins or atoms or genes
    combining accidentally to yield a certain psychic reaction?
Suppose that it springs from an unexplainable seed
    sown in us by the Creator of life,
    bringing purpose,
    giving meaning to each flicker of existence,
    lifting the whole of life.
Suppose too that the universe, and human existence with it,
    is designed for the purpose of glorifying and testifying
    to the marvelous presence of God.
Pursue this possibility, and see your life
    conceived from the love of God
    through the love of man and woman.
Tell me what there is in life besides this love
    that fills your days with joy,
    and leaves you when you turn from its light
    to the darkness of despair and aimlessness.
Explain to me the enormous joke of your life,
    and all human endeavor,
    without the underlying fact of that love;
    tell me the purpose of life without God.

Reprinted with permission from YOUTH Magazine
(February, 1967) published by United Church Press.

TWO

WHO IS THIS MAN JESUS?

I. WHAT FANTASTIC CLAIMS DID JESUS MAKE?
   A. John 14:6

   B. John 10:9

   C. John 10:14

   D. John 10:36

   E. John 11:25

II. WHAT EVIDENCE DID HE PRODUCE TO SUBSTANTIATE HIS CLAIMS?
   A. John 5:36 — What are a few of them?
      1. *Matthew 14:14-21*

      2. *Mark 5:35-41*

      3. *Mark 10:46-52*

      4. *Luke 17:12-19*

      5. *John 11:30-45*

   B. John 5:37 — On what occasions and in what ways did God manifest Himself on Christ's behalf?
      1. *Luke 2:4-16*

      2. *Matthew 2:1,2*

      3. *Mark 1:9-11*

      4. *Matthew 17:1-9*

5. *Matthew 27:50-54*

6. *Matthew 28:1-6*

7. *Luke 24:44-53*

C. John 5:39 — Compare these Old Testament Scriptures with the New Testament references.

1. *Micah 5:2*	1. *Matthew 2:1*
2. *Isaiah 7:14*	2. *Matthew 1:21-23*
3. *Zechariah 13:7*	3. *Mark 14:27*
4. *Isaiah 53:12*	4. *Mark 15:28*
5. *Psalm 22:1*	5. *Mark 15:34*
6. *Psalm 22:18*	6. *John 19:24*
7. *Exodus 12:43,46* *Psalm 34:20 (K.J.V.)*	7. *John 19:32-37 (v.36)*
8. *Zechariah 12:10*	8. *John 19:32-37 (v.37)*
9. *Isaiah 53:7-9 (vs.9)*	9. *Matthew 27:57-60*

There are over 300 Old Testament prophecies that were fulfilled by Jesus Christ.

D. Romans 1:3,4 —

1. *Did He know about his resurrection ahead of time?*
   Matthew 16:21

2. *What precautions were taken to prevent his resurrection?*
   Matthew 27:62-66

3. *Did they work? Matthew 28:1-6; John 20:1-10*

4. *What were some of his post-resurrection appearances?*
   a. *Matthew 28:8-10*

   b. *Mark 16:9-11*

   c. *Mark 16:12 (given in detail in Luke 24:13-33)*

   d. *Mark 16:14*

   e. *Luke 24:36-48*

   f. *I Corinthians 15:3-8*

III. WHAT WERE THE OPINIONS OF HIS CONTEMPORARIES CONCERNING HIM?

A. Peter — Matthew 16:15,16

B. Disciples — Matthew 14:33

C. Philip — John 1:45

D. Nathanael — John 1:49

E. Centurian — Matthew 27:54

F. Pilate — John 19:4

G. Thomas — John 20:24-28

Who do you think He is?

I read
In a book
That a man called
Christ
Went about doing good.

It is very disconcerting to me
That I am so easily
Satisfied
With just
Going about.

—George Small

A ragged cloak on His shoulders
A crown of thorns on His head—
"Here is the Man!"
Abandoned by His friends
* cast off by His people—*
Look at the loser, the victim,
* the scapegoat.*
He has no armies, no advocates,
* scarcely a friend.*
"Here is the Man!"
Alone—yet not lonely.
Beaten—yet undefeated.
Crushed—yet calm.
"Here is the Man!"
And in that one Man, see all men.
In His defeat was born our victory.
"Here is the Man!"

—*James Keller*

* * *

Jesus said unto them: "Who do you say that I am?"

And they replied: "You are the eschatological manifestation of the ground of our being, the kerygma in which we find the ultimate meaning of our interpersonal relationship."

And Jesus said, "What?"

—Found on a graffiti wall at
St. John's University,
Collegeville, Minnesota

Here is a young man who was born in an obscure village,
the child of a peasant woman. He grew up in another village;
He worked in a carpenter shop until he was thirty, and then
for three years he was an itinerant preacher. He never wrote
a book. He never held an office. He never owned a home. He
never had a family. He never went to a college. He never put
his foot inside a big city. He never traveled 200 miles from
the place where he was born. He never did any one of the things
that usualy accompany greatness. He has no credentials but
himself.

While he was still a young man, the tide of public opinion
turned against him. His friends ran away. He was turned over
to his enemies. He went through the mockery of a trial. He
was nailed to a cross between two thieves. While he was dying,
his executioners gambled for the only piece of property he had
on earth and that was his coat.

When he was dead, he was laid in a borrowed grave through
the pity of a friend.

Nineteen centuries wide have come and gone, and today he
is the central figure of the human race and the leader of the
column of progress.

I am far within the mark when I say that all the armies
that ever marched, and all the navies that ever sailed, and
all the parliaments that ever sat, and all the kings that ever
reigned, put together, have not affected the life of man
upon this earth as has that ONE SOLITARY LIFE.

THE HOUND OF HEAVEN

*I fled Him, down the nights and down the days
I fled Him, down the arches of the years
I fled Him, down the labryinthine ways
Of my own mind, and in the midst of tears
I hid from Him.
From those strong feet that followed, followed after
But with unhurrying chase
And unperturbed pace
Deliberate speed, majestic instancy
They beat—and a voice beat more instant than the feet,
"All things betray thee who betrayest Me."*

THREE

ME? A PROBLEM?

I. PROBLEMS WITH MYSELF

Since God loves me, and since He created me, I will:

A. LEARN TO ACCEPT MYSELF THE WAY HE MADE ME.

Read Psalm 139:13,14, preferably from a modern translation.

1. *When we constantly complain about our looks, talents, environment, etc. whom are we really complaining against?*

2. *What does the Bible say God thinks about complaining? Numbers 11:1*

B. LEARN TO BE HONEST WITH MYSELF

1. *God sees me as I am. Read Jeremiah 17:10*

2. *Others see me as I am. Proverbs 20:11*

3. *In view of this, what is a good daily prayer for me to pray? Psalm 139:23,24*

C. LEARN TO BE HONEST WITH GOD

Read Psalm 139:1-12, preferably from a modern translation.

1. *Where did David think about hiding from God?*

2. *How do we sometimes try to hide from Him?*

3. *What reward do we have for being honest with God? Psalm 66:18-20*

D. LEARN TO ACCEPT EACH DAY AS IT COMES

1. *What did Paul say he had learned? Philippians 4:11-13*

2. *What is the command of Philippians 4:4?*

3. What are the steps to rejoicing always? Philippians 4:6

   a.

   b.

   c.

4. What then is the result? Verse 7

5. What can we count on God to do if we trust, pray, and praise? Philippians 4:19

6. What are some qualifying factors in prayer?

   a. James 4:3

   b. Psalm 37:4

Talking to You seems so strange, Lord
My voice bounces off the walls.
Do You really hear?

War, street riots, dope.
Lord, my world is falling apart!
Do You really care?

At home, at church, at school
Lord, I'm three people
Do You really know who I am?

Salvation, forgiveness, abundant life,
Lord, they're more than words—aren't they?
Lord, help me to be who You want me to be
Not someday—NOW.

Help me to live and not pretend at living.
Help me to love and not be swallowed up
   by sex.
Help me to care and not keep track of my
   expense.

Take my restless, yearning spirit, Lord,
And make it yours.
Take my insecurity and me.
Set me free, free O Lord, to belong to You.

> —Donald A. Leigh

Lord of All,
You planned
this new day
A million years ago
That I might
Watch
its sunrise
And start
again!
Thank You, Lord.

> *—Dolores Carus*

GAMES WE PLAY

YOU DON'T UNDERSTAND ME! This game is usually played with one or more parents and proves to be the greatest challenge if the parents are over 50. This is because they are old, on the verge of senility and really out of touch with the Now Generation. The key player in this game is the teen-ager; the object of the game is to convince the parent that he is wrong and could never possibly understand teen problems. This creates a situation where the parent throws in the sponge and the grownup-to-be wins the right to take out membership in the Never Trust Anyone Over 30 Club.

> *—Jim Smoke*

Wondrous God,
When I have finished
planning
and organizing
and worrying
And the situation
Seems impossible —
Do it Your way!
. . . . . . .and forgive me!

> —Dolores Carus

FOUR

MOODS

I. WHAT IS GOD'S SOLUTION TO EACH MOOD OR EMOTION?
   A. LONELINESS
      1. *Matthew 28:20*

      2. *Hebrews 13:5b*

   B. FEARFULNESS
      1. *Psalm 56:3*

      2. *Psalm 34:7*

      3. *Psalm 4:8*

      4. *Psalm 27:1*

   C. WORRY
      1. *Matthew 6:25-34*

   D. HEAVY-HEARTEDNESS
      1. *Psalm 55:22*

      2. *Matthew 11:28-30*

      3. *Isaiah 43:1,2*

II. GOD'S WAY OUT
   A. What does the Bible say about happiness?
      1. *Proverbs 17:22*

      2. *Proverbs 15:15*

   B. Where is the Christians' source of joy? Psalm 16:8-11

C. What does God's joy become for us? Nehemiah 8:10b

D. What is especially pleasing to God?
   1. *Psalm 50:23*

   2. *Colossians 2:7*

   3. *Ephesians 5:19*

   4. *If you can't do that, what can you do? Psalm 100:1*

THE SOLITARY WAY

There is a mystery in human
  hearts
And though we be encircled by
  a host
Of those who love us well, and
  are beloved,
To every one of us, from time to
  time
There comes a sense of utter
  loneliness.
Our dearest friend is stranger
  to our joy,
And canot realize our bitterness.
"There is not one who really
  understands
No one to enter in to all I feel."
Such is the cry of each of us. In
  turn
We wander in a solitary way.

No matter what or where our
  lot may be
Each heart, mysterious even to
  itself,
Must live its inner life in
  solitude.
And would you know the reason
  why this is?
It is because the Lord desires
  our love.
In every heart He wishes to be
  first.
He therefore keeps the secret

key Himself,
To open all its chambers, and
  to bless
With perfect sympathy, and
  holy peace
Each solitary soul which comes
  to Him.

So when we feel this loneliness
It is the voice of Jesus saying,
    "Come to Me."
And every time we are not
  understood
It is a call to us to come again:
For Christ alone can satisfy the
  soul,
And those who walk with Him
  from day to day
Can never have a "solitary way."

And when beneath some heavy
  cross you faint,
And say, "I cannot bear this
  load alone,"
You say the truth . . . Christ
  made it purposely
So heavy that you must return
  to Him.
The bitter grief, which "no one
  understands,"
Conveys a secret message from
  the King
Entreating you to come again.

The "Man or Sorrows" understands it well,
"In all points" tempted
He can feel with you.
You cannot come too often or too near.
The Son of God is infinite in grace,
His presence satisfies the longing soul
And those who walk with Him from day to day,
Can never have a "solitary way."

AND THEN CAME LAUGHTER

And then came Laughter.
Laughter to heal the wounded;
Laughter to hearten the disillusioned;
Laughter to bring sunshine during a storm
Laughter to bring music to each day.

Then came Love
Love that stirs dying flames,
And causes tides to turn
And roses to bloom.
Love that brings happiness to each season.

Then came Green
Green in the swaying trees;
Green in blooming flowers,
And the Green in grass, sparkling with morning's dew.
And the Green in someone's joy-filled eyes.

Then came Loneliness.
Loneliness that comes with the dark;
Loneliness that fills each hour,
Each day, each minute, each second
That I live without Your presence.

—Denese Mott

Written shortly after becoming a Christian as the expression
of her new relationship.

Old is lonely, God
There's an old man
down the street, Lord—
    You know him—
just stares through
    his mornings into nights.
Wonder if he's thinking
    all the time?
Probably sleeps a lot.
Young is lonely, too, God,
    but it's a different breed
    and offers more cures.
Could young lonely
cure old lonely
    and work the other way
    around?
—Lois Breiner

GAMES WE PLAY

*I'D REALLY LIKE TO GO OUT
WITH YOU BUT . . .*
*This is strictly a boy-girl contest.
One must be eager, the other
belligerent. The object is to
convince the opposite player
that you really do like him (her)
and would just love to date
him (her) but your schedule
is so full of studying and help-
ing around the house that you
just don't have time. The out-
come is usually a crushed spirit
and a relieved spirit.*

—*Jim Smoke*

FIVE

ME AND MY PARENTS

I. SINCE GOD LOVES MY PARENTS AND HAS MADE THEM RESPONSIBLE FOR ME, I WILL:

Learn to accept them the way they are. Accept their failures and mistakes and love them anyway. If I run short of love, I must ask God for His. (He has plenty to spare).

1. *What does the Apostle Paul tell Timothy in I Timothy 4:12?*

   a.

   b.

2. *What are the characteristics of true love? I Corinthians 13:4-7 (Use a modern translation)*

B. LEARN TO OBEY MY PARENTS. (God commands it).

1. *What two things should young people give their parents? Ephesians 6:1,2*

   a.

   b.

   (A rare exception to the rule might be an occasional non-Christian parent who might ask a young person to do something contrary to God's Word, but even non-Christian parents should be respected and obeyed). Read I Peter 2:18-21. Can this be applied to your relationship?

2. *Whom are we really trying to please? Colossians 3:20-24*

C. TRY TO COMMUNICATE WITH MY PARENTS

Resentment and hostility breed resentment and hostility.

1. *Write out Proverbs 15:1*

2. *Learn to listen without resentment. What does the writer of Proverbs call a youth who refuses to take advice from his parents? Proverbs 15:5*

3. *Try to help make the atmosphere in your home one of mutual love and respect. What does God want in our homes?*

   a. *Ephesians 4:31,32*

   b. *I Peter 3:8-11*

   c. *Colossians 3:13,14*

4. *Who supplies what when things get rough?*

   a. *II Corinthians 12:9,10*

LOVE IS:
very patient and kind,
never jealous or envious,
never boastful or proud,
never haughty or selfish or rude.
Love does not demand its own
  way,
It is not irritable or touchy.
It does not hold grudges
  and will hardly even notice
  when others do it wrong.
It is never glad about injustice,
  but rejoices whenever truth
  wins out.
If you love someone you will be
  loyal to him
    no matter what the cost.
You will always believe in him,
  always expect the best of him
  and always stand your ground
    in defending him.
Love goes on forever.

The Living Bible
I Corinthians 13:4-8

GAMES WE PLAY

MOM (OR DAD), YOU ARE THE GREATEST! This game is also called "setting up your parents." It usually involves all the players in a home with the object being to inflate parental ego enough for the young "Jacob" to win a large prize—the family car for the weekend, some new clothes, ten dollars for a date, extended curfew hours or just plain getting what I want. Other children in the home can play this game also. The action is intensified after one child gets a prize; the others are thus enabled to exert pressure by accusing the parents of partiality if all the players don't get a prize. The game usually ends with the parents being taken to the cleaners.

—Jim Smoke

And as we live with Christ
  Our love grows more perfect and complete;
  so we will not be ashamed and embarrased
    at the day of judgment,
  but we can face Him with confidence and joy,
  because He loves us and we love Him too.
We need have no fear of someone who loves perfectly;
  his perfect love for us eliminates all dread
    of what he might do to us.
If we are afraid, it is for fear of what he might do to us,
  and shows that we are not fully convinced
  that he really loves us.
So you see, our love for him
  comes as a result
  of his loving us first.
If anyone says "I love God,"
  but keeps on hating his brother,
  he is a liar;
for if he doesn't love his brother who is
  right there in front of him,
how can he love God whom
  he has never seen?
And God himself has said that one must love
  not only God,
  but his brother too.

The Living Bible
I John 4:17-21

SIX

GOD HAS A PLAN

I. GOD HAS PROMISED TO GUIDE HIS CHILDREN

   A. In the following verses, what is God's promise? What is our part?

      1. *Psalm 32:8,9*

      2. *Proverbs 3:5,6*

      3. *John 10:3,4*

II. START WHERE I AM

   I must ask for forgivenes for past sins and mistakes and put them behind me.

   A. What does God do with forgiven sins?

      1. *Psalm 103:12*

      2. *Isaiah 44:22*

   B. What are we now in Christ? II Corinthians 5:17

   C. What did the Apostle Paul do about his past? Philippians 3:13,14

III. RECOGNIZE GOD'S GUIDANCE IS FOR "THE DAY", "THE STEP", "THE HOUR"

   Read Psalm 37:23

IV. REALIZE THAT GOD'S WAYS AND OUR WAYS ARE VASTLY DIFFERENT.

   A. What is the difference between our ideas and God's? Isaiah 55:8,9

   B. What should we guard against? Ecclesiastes 5:2 Jeremiah 10:23

C. What is the important thing to the Lord? I Samuel 15:22,23

D. What is necessary in discerning God's will? Psalm 119:105

V. LEARN TO "LISTEN" TO THE HOLY SPIRIT.
How did God speak to Elijah? I Kings 19:9-12

"In quietness and confidence shall be your strength." Isaiah 30:15

VI. LINE UP THESE THREE THINGS

A. THE WORD "Is my decision in keeping with God's revealed will?"

B. CIRCUMSTANCES "Walk toward 'open doors,' asking God to 'close' those not in His will for you." Acts 15:27. "Don't barge into a 'closed' door." Acts 16:7

C. INNER PEACE

Lord Jesus, when I
asked You to
open the doors, to
show me ways to
serve You and
Your own, and to
seek those
who are not, I
didn't know so many
doors would open
so wide, nor
that stepping
through them I
would find
so much
to do; nor that
all of it
would be
so exciting . . .
Great Carpenter,
build those
doors daily, put
them before me,
and then
give me the
strength to step
through them,
I pray.

  —Dolores Carus

Ye call me Master and obey me not
Ye call me Light and see me not
Ye call me Way and walk me not
Ye call me Life and desire me not
Ye call me Wise and follow me not
Ye call me Fair and love me not
Ye call me Rich and ask me not
Ye call me Eternal and seek me not
Ye call me Gracious and trust me not
Ye call me Noble and serve me not
Ye call me Mighty and honor me not
Ye call me Just and fear me not
If I condemn you, blame me not.

  —Found engraved on an old slab in the
  Cathedral of Lubeck, Germany

GAMES WE PLAY

BUT EVERYONE ELSE IS GOING! This game pits the discretion and cunning of parents against the awesome mass of young people who are going, doing or wearing "it." The goal is to convince the parents that the majority is always right. After all, how could that many people possibly be wrong? This game usually lasts many days and is played in five-minute intervals, several times a day, usually before and after school and at the dinner table. It sometimes involves yelling and tears and much misunderstanding. It is very difficult for the parents to win this game.

  —Jim Smoke

NO TIME FOR GOD

No time for God?
What fools we are to clutter up
Our lives with common things
And leave without the hearts gate,
The Lord of life, and life itself—

No time for God?
That day when sickness comes,
Or trouble finds you out,
And you cry out to God,
Will He have time for you?

SEVEN

I AM RESPONSIBLE

I. TO GOD: TO KEEP MY BODY AND MIND PURE AND HOLY
Give the main message of each verse.
   1. *I Corinthians 6:19,20*

   2. *I John 3:2-4*

   3. *Philippians 4:8*

   4. *I Peter 1:14-16*

II. TO CHRISTIAN FRIENDS:
A. TO HAVE FELLOWSHIP
   1. *What two things do we have by walking in the light?
   I John 1:7*

      a.

      b.

   2. *What should we do, and what should we not do in our
   relationship with others?*

      a. Hebrews 10:24

      b. Hebrews 10:25

      c. Hebrews 10:25

B. TO SHOW LOVE
   1. *How are we to love? I Peter 1:22*

   2. *How do we show love?*

      a. Galatians 6:9,10

      b. Matthew 25:34-46

C. **TO PRAY WITH AND FOR THEM**
What does James say we should do? James 5:16
1.

2.

What kind of prayer works? (same verse)

D. **TO RECOGNIZE WE ARE ALL IMPORTANT IN GOD'S WORK**
   1. *What is Paul trying to tell us in I Corinthians 12:12-31*

   2. *What should be our attitude toward fellow Christians? Philippians 2:3,4*

E. **TO BE CAREFUL NO ONE STUMBLES BECAUSE OF ME**
State briefly five guidelines for Christain behavior.
   1. *Romans 14:1*

   2. *Romans 14:13*

   3. *Romans 14:16*

   4. *Romans 14:19*

   5. *Romans 14:22*

''Each time I take the wheel,
Oh Lord, I pray,
Grant that no harm shall come
Of me today.
See over hills for me,
On curves stand by,
Post some bright Angel near
To see that I
Observe the playing child,
The old, less spry;
No act of mine must cause
Someone to die.''

GAMES WE PLAY
I REALLY LIKE THIS CLASS
AND YOU ARE A GREAT TEACH-
ER BUT . . . This game is some-
times called "snow job." It involves
a teacher and a student and is
usually played when a homework
assignment or term paper is due
to be turned in. The object is to
make the teacher feel good and
get an extension for the overdue
assignment. The game usually
starts when there are more ex-
citing things to do than homework.
It ends when the student is
marked down for the late assign-
ment.

—*Jim Smoke*

Because you belong to Christ
You are akin to me
One in the bonds unbreakable—
Wrought for eternity
Spirit with spirit twined—
Who can the knot undo
Binding the Christ within my
   heart
Unto the Christ in you.

† †

Bread of God
train me not to
ruin my appetite
for You
by filling up on the goodies
and the trash
of this world.

—Nancy Spiegelberg

From DECISION ©1973 by the
Billy Graham Evangelistic Association

''*Those who attempt new flights*
   often fall
Failure consists not in the fall
   but in the refusal to fly
   again.''

† †

Walls of fear built up inside
Were broken down with a smile
Sudden light on darkened mind
And all you did was smile.
Confidence built up again
When you bothered to smile
Such a simple gesture meant a
   world to me
Because along the way
You stopped to smile.

—*Arlin Seashore*

EIGHT

REACHING OUT

I AM RESPONSIBLE TO NON-CHRISTIANS
   A. NOT TO TAKE PART IN THEIR SIN
   What is God's command concerning this?
      1. Proverbs 1:10

      2. II Corinthians 6:16-18

   B. NOT TO BE ASHAMED OF BEING A CHRISTIAN
   What is it important to do? Why?
      1. Matthew 10:32,33

      2. Romans 10:9,10

      3. Romans 10:13,14

   C. TO HAVE A GOOD TESTIMONY
   How can we do this?
      1. Colossians 4:5,6

      2. I John 2:4-6

   D. TO SHOW LOVE
   How important is this?
      1. I John 2:8-11

      2. II Peter 1:5-9

   E. TO BRING THEM TO CHRIST
      1. What disciples were examples of this and whom did they bring? John 1:40, 41, 45

2. Give another example. John 4:28-30

3. What promise is there for us? Acts 1:8

LISTEN CHRISTIAN

I was hungry
and you formed
a humanities club
and discussed my hunger.
Thank you.

I was imprisoned
and you crept off quietly
to your chapel in the cellar
and prayed for my release.

I was naked,
and in your mind
you debated the morality
of my appearance.

I was sick
and you knelt and thanked God
for your health.

I was homeless
and you preached to me
of the spiritual shelter
of the love of God.

I was lonely
and you left me alone
to pray for me.

You seem so holy;
so close to God.
But I'm still very hungry
and lonely
and cold . . .

—Bob Rowland

GAMES WE PLAY

GUESS WHAT HAPPENED TO THE CAR. This is a game of translation. The parents try to guess what really happened by the anguished look on the son's or daughter's face. Usually a nervous, happy, gleeful, chuckling attitude is translated into a dented fender, bumper or paint scratch. A blank, somber, downcast look translates anything more than $50 damage. Running to your room and hiding under the bed usually means you dropped the transmission dragging out of the hamburger joint. The ultimate goal of this game is to convince your parents it wasn't your fault so that you don't have to pay the repair bill.

—Jim Smoke

NINE

GOD UNDERSTANDS

I. GOD KNOWS MY WEAKNESSES
   A. What is His attitude toward His children?
      1. *Psalm 103:13-15*

II. GOD KNOWS MY CIRCUMSTANCES
   A. What is He aware of?
      1. *Exodus 2:23-25; Exodus 3:7-10*

      2. *John 1:43-49*

      3. *I Kings 19:9*

      4. *Revelation 2:2,9,13,19 (Pick out one or two things from each verse)*

III. GOD KNOWS MY HEART
   A. Why does God's opinion of us differ from what people think?
      1. *I Samuel 16:7*

      2. *Jeremiah 17:10*

IV. GOD KNOWS MY TRIALS
   A. Why does God allow hard things to come into our lives?
      1. *John 9:1-3*

      2. *Hebrews 12:5-11 (re-read verse 10)*

V. GOD KNOWS ABOUT MY TEMPTATIONS

A. Why can Jesus understand our temptations?
   1. *Hebrews 4:15*

   2. *Hebrews 2:18*

B. What does this mean to me?
   1. *Hebrews 4:16*

C. Are all our problems God's fault?
   1. *Where does a large part of the blame lie? Galatians 6:7,8*

   2. *How are we tempted? James 1:12-17*

   3. *Who is the instigator of temptation? II Corinthians 2:11, Acts 5:3*

   4. *What is he compared to? What does this suggest?*
      a. II Corinthians 11:14

      b. I Peter 5:8,9

VI. GOD'S SOLUTION TO TEMPTATION
   A. Realize that everyone is subject to it. I Peter 5:9, I Corinthians 10:13
      1. *What is God's promise in I Corinthians 10:12,13*

      2. *What do we need to do? James 4:6-10*

      3. *Certain sins we are told to avoid or run from. What are they and why are we told to "run" from these particular sins?*
         a. I Corinthians 10:14

         b. I Corinthians 6:18

         c. II Timothy 2:22

         d. I Timothy 6:10,11

         How do we "run" from them?

   B. It *is* possible to come out on top.
      Where is our Help? How great is it?

1. *I Corinthians 15:57*

2. *Ephesians 3:20,21*

3. *I John 4:4; 5:4*

With five fingers on each hand, five toes on each foot, and five senses, sight, hearing, taste, touch and smell, they can constantly remind us of important truth the Bible teaches, as vital to our well-being spiritually, as our senses and our physical members.

Here are the *five universal principles of Christian behavior.* Master them, to be blessed and be a blessing to others every day of your life. For a full explanation of their importance see Kenneth O. Gangel, *The Family First,* pp 95-98, published by His International Service.

The principles are: *body control* — I Corinthians 6:13-20; *self-edification* — I Corinthians 10:23; *habit freedom* — I Corinthians 6:12; *life-testimony* — I Corinthians 8; and *Christ pre-eminence* — Colossians 1:18.

Our bodies are the Lord's and Christ indwells them, so that the Christian becomes a temple and the body is not to be defiled;

we are to choose what builds us up, what is unquestionably good for us, not what tears us down;

living on the higher plane Christ empowers us to live, we have a freedom so superior it is a wonder we can be tempted to accept anything less than God's best, or seek a mere religious compliance with minimum requirements of nominal Christianity;

we can have such a joy that even a desire not strictly forbidden will gladly be given up to prevent some weaker, misunderstanding Christian from questioning our walk;

and giving Christ first place, the "not I but Christ" standard of holy, happy, fruitful Christian living is seen to be the normal Christian life.

Nothing is more important for us to learn if we are to be victorious over life's common dangers and pitfalls.

*   *   *

Love has a hem in its garment
That reaches the very dust
It can touch the stains   I am but one
Of the streets and lanes   But I am one
And because it can, it must.   I cannot do everything
I ought to bend to the lowest   But I can do something
I ought, and therefore, I can   What I can do
I was made to the end   I should do
That I might descend   And what I should do
In the steps of the Son of Man.   By God's grace I will do.

No one is beat till he quits
No one is through till he stops
No matter how hard failure hits
No matter how often he drops
No one is down . . . til he lies
In the dirt and refuses to rise.

◆

They call him a diamond
in the rough
he calls himself a believer
I'm not sure what You call him
or what I think of him either
but here he is
Your creation
I'm bringing him to You
in Christian love
and in obedience to Your will.
If he has to be polished
please God
You run the buffer.
—Norma E. Smith
From DECISION, © 1973
Billy Graham Evangelistic Association

Got up this morning
He was on my mind
I've got troubles
I've got worries
I've got wounds to bind

Went to the Bible
Just to read His Word
Read He loved me
Read He suffered
Read He died for me

I've got a feeling
Way down in my heart
He'll take my troubles
He'll take my worries
He'll take my wounds to
   bind

Got up this morning
He was on my mind
No more troubles
No more worries
No more wounds to
   bind.
—Gamble Folk Singers

GAMES WE PLAY

MY TEACHER DOESN'T LIKE ME! This game is always played at report card time. The ingredients for this game are: one .. student, one teacher, one or two parents, and any number of grades below C level. The object is to pit the teacher against the parents and convince both that a great injustice has been done to the student. The goal of course, is to prevent the parents from putting the son or daughter on restriction for the next nine weeks.

—Jim Smoke

WITHOUT A SONG

Filling our heads with mind
  wanderings,
  so many thoughts like unsorted
laundry
   and broken cans,
listening to anything
   sopping up the world's
  man sounds
    frenzied
    gagging
    gnashing sounds
and alowing our mouths
to utter anything
   anything at all
defaming
cursing
lying
   (who hears?)
    and then we wonder,
    Why doesn't heaven
     sing
    in our souls?

Mind Things, by Marie Chapian, © 1973
Creation House, Carol Stream, Illinois

TEN

DANGERS AND PITFALLS

I. TRUTH vs. FALSEHOOD

Where there is truth, there is the false.
Where there is reality, there is the artificial.

A. What does Jesus warn us about in Matthew 24:4,5,23 and 24?

B. What is the Apostle Paul's warning to Timothy in II Timothy 4:3,4?

C. Where is truth found? John 17:17

D. Who is truth? John 1:14; John 14:6

II. TESTING THE TRUTH

A. What do they think of Jesus Christ? I John 2:21-25

B. Is it true to the Scriptures? What are the consequences of not being true to the Word of God?

1. *Proverbs 30:5,6*

2. *Revelation 22:18,19*

III. THE FALSENESS OF THE OCCULT

A. Read Deuteronomy 18:9-14 from a modern translation, if possible. What things are warned against?

B. What are these things in the eyes of God? Vs. 12

C. What does Isaiah 8:19,20 say?

D. What sin of the occult is mentioned in Galatians 5:19-21

E. God's final judgment against those practicing the occult is found in Revelation 21:8 and 22:15. Read and note its severity.

F. Read II Corinthians 6:14-18

   1. *What is God's will for the Christian?*

   2. *What is His promise?*

IV. WHAT ABOUT DRINKING?

A. A "favorite" verse of many people who know little else about the Bible is I Timothy 5:23. Why was this advice given to Timothy? Compare it to Romans 14:21,22. What must a Christian always take into consideration?

B. Read each of the following verses and give the warning.
   1. *Isaiah 5:11*

   2. *Proverbs 20:1*

   3. *Proverbs 23:19-21*

   4. *Proverbs 23:29-35*

C. Who especially should not drink? Proverbs 31:4-7

D. What are Christians to God? Revelation 1:5,6

E. What are the two commands of Ephesians 5:18?

If this is your problem—there is deliverance for you through Jesus Christ. Do you feel like Paul did in Romans 7:15-25? Move on and live in Romans 8:1,2

WHY DRINK?

THE TERRIBLE TOLL

"O God, they say that gasoline and liquor do not mix," a grieving woman wrote after her granddaughter was killed by a drinking driver. "But we as a family have learned that they do. They mix with flesh and blood and dirt and gravel and sand and steel and stone."

Now this may surprise you. The greatest peril on the highway is not the drunk. "Social drinkers, not alcoholics, account for most accidents involving drunken driving," says Raymond K. Berg, presiding judge of the Chicago Traffic Court.

One or two beers or cocktails lower inhibitions. A driver is willing to take more risks, drive faster, take a chance on passing when the road isn't clear ahead. With three or four drinks, judgment slows and coordination weakens. Thinking is muddled. With five or six, vision is blurred. With seven or eight, the driver is seeing double, losing his balance.

In a mile of driving you may need to make as many as 200 observations and 20 decisions. Unable to think clearly, the drinking driver is a rolling bomb.

YOUR OWN WORST ENEMY

Hundreds of drinkers are casualties in off-the-highway accidents. A study of 50 accident fatalities among Metropolitan Life Insurance policyholders lists these facts:

Half of the poisoning victims died by taking sleeping pills and alcohol in combination.

One-fifth of the accidental deaths caused by inhalation of poisonous gas and vapors were charged to drink.

A fifth of the deaths due to fires and burns from careless smoking probably wouldn't have happened if the victims hadn't been drinking.

Besides home accidents, hundreds of thousands of people are killed or maimed in accidents at work because of drinking.

How fitting is the little rhyme:
I do not think that I should drink,
For if I drink, I do not think.

SCOTCH ON THE ROCKS

The United States Public Health Service estimates that 70% of all divorces (715,000 in 1970) are caused in part by alcohol abuse.

Drinking also causes money problems that lead to family break-ups. And to bitter quarrels, fights that culminate in physical violence and, too often, to physically abused children.

TERRIBLE TALLY

The misery and sorrow resulting from drinking cannot be accurately tallied in dollars and cents. But the National Institute on Alcohol Abuse estimates the cost at $25 billion each year. That includes about $9 billion cost to U.S. industry and another $5 billion to government agencies because of drunken employees.

The total is more than the $14.7 billion actually spent for alcohol by Americans each year. This is twice the amount given to religion and welfare!

And some people have the nerve to say, "Look at all the benefits we get from taxes placed on alcohol."

UNMASKING THE MYTHS

No one denies that alcohol has worthwhile uses in industry and medicine. But there are some myths about beverage alcohol that need discounting.

Myth 1—*Alcohol stimulates the brain and makes a person think more clearly.* Wrong. It depresses and dulls the brain.

Myth 2—*A drink or two makes a person braver.* No, it only makes him foolhardy. It deadens the nervous system, stifling the alarm or fatigue that he would normally feel.

Myth 3—*Drinking makes a person warmer.* The drinker's skin feels warm and his face may be flushed. But alcohol jams the body's natural thermostat and drains away natural heat. Doctors warn against drinking when exposed to extremely cold weather.

Myth 4—*Alcoholic beverages are desirable for use as medicine.* The American Medical Association officially opposes the use of alcoholic beverages as a medicine.

Myth 5—*All important people drink.* This is an illusion created by slick ads and commercials. Hundreds of "Who's Who" type persons in all fields are total abstainers. Coach Tom Landry of the Dallas Cowboys football team is one. Anita Bryant is another. Governor Reubin Askew of Florida does not drink and never serves alcoholic beverages at official receptions.

Myth 6—*You must drink on certain occasions or you would offend your host.* Abstaining may displease some hosts, but etiquette authority Amy Vanderbilt says only a poor host will insist on guests drinking. William Cameron Townsend, founder of the Wycliffe Bible Translators, has been honored at dozens of presidential banquets in Latin American countries. He has always said no to alcohol in favor of juice or water. Recently at a banquet in Russia he was praised as the "only American we've ever known to turn down alcohol."

YOUR DECISION

Hopefully, you are one who believes in thinking for yourself. Since no sane person encourages excessive drinking, there is only one possible choice open.

Abstain. This means if you've started drinking, stop. If you have never imbibed, don't start. Says Ann Landers: "This is the only sure way of never becoming an alcoholic, of never hurting anyone else while under the influence of alcohol."

—By James C. Hefley

ELEVEN

THE SOURCE OF POWER

I. THE FRUIT OF THE SPIRIT

A. What kind of fruit is talked about in Proverbs 11:30?

B. What is the fruit of the Spirit as given in Galatians 5:22,23?

II. THE FILLING OF THE SPIRIT

A. When do we receive the Holy Spirit? Romans 8:9; I Corinthians 12:13; Galatians 4:6

B. What is the command of Ephesians 5:18?

C. What is the result of a Spirit-filled life? Ephesians 5:19-21
   a _________________ heart; a _________________ heart;
   a _________________ spirit.

D. What is another result of being filled with the Spirit? Acts 1:8

E. Steps to being filled with the Spirit.

   1. *Self Examination — Am I really born again? How does II Corinthians 13:5 state it?*

   2. *Confess All Known Sin — If we confess, what will God do? I John 1:9*

   3. *Yield Fully To God — What does God want our bodies to be? Romans 12:1,2*

   4. *Ask To Be Filled — What is the promise of Luke 11:9-13?*

   5. *Thank Him For It — When we ask for something and have met the conditions, what must we believe? Hebrews 11:6*

6. *Abide In Christ — What is necessary to being a fruit-bearing Christian? John 15:1-10*

III. FOLLOWING THROUGH

Since the Holy Spirit is a person it is possible to hinder His work in us.

A. What is the warning of Ephesians 4:30?

B. What is the command of I Thessalonians 5:19?

We "grieve" the Holy Spirit when we refuse to deal with sin in our lives and we "quench" or "smother" Him when we are disobedient to Him.

Don't pray for more of the Spirit . . . pray that He will have more of you.

Remember the Holy Spirit's job is always to GLORIFY JESUS CHRIST. John 16:13,14

Is Jesus Christ being glorified in YOUR life?

HE PRAYED

He prayed for strength that he might achieve;
He was made weak that he might obey.
He prayed for health that he might do great things;
He was given infirmity that he might do better things.
He prayed for riches that he might be happy;
He was given poverty that he might be wise.
He prayed for power that he might have the praise of men;
He was given weakness that he might feel the need of God.
He prayed for all things that he might enjoy life;
He was given life that he might enjoy all things.
He had received nothing that he asked for—all that he hoped for;
His prayer was answered—he was most blessed.

I tried
to do the work of God.
I had so many
good ideas . . .
great plans . . .
enthusiasm . . .
but I failed.

And in that failure
learned a lesson rare.
God's work
must be done
by God's Spirit.

I only need be
clean,
available,
and filled with Him
so He can do
His work
through me.

—Gladys Seashore

"Not by might nor by power,
but by my Spirit, saith the Lord
of Hosts." Zechariah 4:6

"Without me
ye can do
nothing." —Jesus

Take time to think
   It is the source of power
Take time to play
   It is the secret of perpetual
     youth
Take time to read
   It is the fountain of wisdom
Take time to pray
   It is the greatest power on
     earth
Take time to love and be loved
   It is a God-given privilege
Take time to be friendly
   It is the road to happiness
Take time to laugh
   It is the music of the soul
Take time to give
   It is too short a day to be
     selfish
Take time to work
   It is the price of success.

TWELVE

THE REASON FOR IT ALL

I. GOD'S IMMEDIATE PURPOSE FOR MY LIFE

  A. What do I need to remind myself of constantly? II Corinthians 5:15

  B. In this world a Christian is to be:
    1. *Matthew 5:13*

    2. *Matthew 5:14*

    3. *II Corinthians 3:2,3*

    4. *I Corinthians 3:9*

    5. *I Corinthians 6:19,20*

    6. *John 15:5,8*

    Salt needs to penetrate
    a light must shine
    the letter must be easy to read
    the laborer must work
    the garden must grow and produce
    the building must have a good foundation
    a temple must glorify its maker
    the branch must abide in the vine
    that it might PRODUCE FRUIT

II. GOD'S ULTIMATE PURPOSE

  A. Read Ephesians 1:9-12 and state what you think God's eternal purpose is for those who love Him.

  B. How will Christ present us to God? Jude 24,25

  C. What are we now waiting for? I Thessalonians 4:16-18

D. Are you ready for His coming? Hebrews 9:28,29

E. What are we told to do? Matthew 24:42-44

F. Why has Christ delayed His coming? II Peter 3:8,9

G. What will our "watching" do for us? II Peter 3:14; I John 3:2,3

H. When will He come? Matthew 24:36

At Christmas Island
And in Siberia
And in Bikini
And in Nevada
Scientists count seconds:
* ten—*
*   nine—*
*   eight—*
*   seven—*
*   six—*
*   five—*
*   four—*
*   three—*
*   two—*
*   one—*
*   (then)*
*   ZERO*
In heaven
Methinks Gabriel must have
   trumpet to lips,
And God be counting;
I hold my breath —
Aye, the whole world holds its
   breath —
Will God be soon saying,
ZERO?

—Tokyo Mailsack

. . . and then there's music!

Well . . . there's good news and bad news . . . they always say, and usually more bad than good.

There's the national and international scene . . . no, that's a bad place to begin. Sounds like a dirge, and who can sing to that?

Sports? No cheery word there . . . the tennis coach says I'm a natural for baseball. What did he mean by that?

The "school of my choice" did not reciprocate. A "surplus of more qualified applicants" was their only reason for turning me down.

No kiss on the first date from Elaine . . . fortunately. She scares me a little anyway.

My refund from IRS better hurry so I can circulate again . . . there are several qualified candidates for romance who ought not be deprived of my attentions for too long.

George Nichols says Jesus Loves me.

What's that doing in there!?!

The truth is, I've heard "Jesus loves you" so many times I half-forget what it means.

But, wow! when I start to think . . . . Sometimes I lose hold on how exciting the Gospel really is. When that happens, I need to get it back to its simplest terms. Why did those early Christians call it Good News?

In those times there were no books, no telephones. Mail wasn't too reliable. The Good News which Jesus brought to an obscure province of the Roman Empire had to be passed by word of mouth.

Amazingly, it was. It spread on and on until it covered the known world. Why? Because it was exciting. Jolting. The Good News was a kind of music that starts your foot to tapping. Listen . . . .

The Good News says God is love.

Most people believe in some kind of God, some big and powerful force that made the universe, guiding planets and making atoms whirl.

The Good News is that God is a Person. He cries over the girl who's pregnant but not married. He shares the sorrow of the guy who's lonely but doesn't trust anyone enough to really talk about it. He's happy when you pull the right answer out of the back of your head.

"Let Him have all your worries and cares, for He is always thinking about you." (1 Peter 5:7)

The Good News says the mighty force that started the universe could be encased in a man, and in fact was the man Jesus. He knows what we go through— He's been there. And He knows we can be better, with God's power — because He lived that power.

". . . for His suffering made Jesus a perfect Leader, one fit to bring people into their salvation." (Hebrews 2:10)

The Good News says everything important about God can be seen in Jesus Christ. That shows immediately the most important thing about God isn't His power or size, because Jesus, by anyone's standards, wasn't big or powerful.

Jesus was, for instance, humble. He never forced Himself on the people He met. The choice was up to them. Even when they were in the process of beating Him and killing Him, He didn't intervene. He cared about them—He said, "Father, forgive them." And today, Jesus still doesn't force Himself on us.

The Good News says God is unreasonably, almost absurdly, forgiving. You might expect God to forgive people for kicking Him around if they groveled a little. It feels good to forgive the kid you've got under your thumb — as long as he stays there, his nose in the dirt.

But Jesus, the God-man didn't require the woman caught in sin to say anything about how sorry she was. Unlike the Puritans, He didn't pin a scarlet letter on her. Before she said a single word He sent her away forgiven. And Jesus talked about how the loving Father doesn't even give His runaway son time to finish his apologies before He starts celebrating his return.

"God chose us to be His very own, through what Christ would do for us; He decided then to make us holy in His eyes, without a single fault — we who stand before Him covered with His love." (Ephesians 1:4)

The Good News says you don't have to be a genius to find right answers to your problems. To solve the problems of your mixed-up world you'd think a complex, mind-bending answer ought to be necessary. The Bible says that's wrong — the Way may not be easy, but it is simple. Anyone can understand it and live it. It simply requires you to shift your allegiance. Instead of serving yourself, you decide to serve God.

The Good News says there is a reason to live. We have a job to do — a job the whole universe is aching to have finished. There's a point to it all — behind those stars and the sun that wakes you every morning is a God whose name is Love . . . and He's your Father.

That's Good News
    to a girl who's sick of being alone on weekends.
    to a guy who's tried out for every sport in school . . . and been cut.
    to a kid who studies hard, but barely manages C's.
    The whole thing is good news!
    Turn it up.
    Turn up the music, my foot's tapping.

—Franklin Potts

Reprinted from *Campus Life* © 1973
Youth For Christ International. Used by permission.

NOTES